THE TRUTH ABOUT A LIE

Tiffany Kameni

SAVE YOUR TIME. SAVE YOUR FAMILY. SAVE YOURSELF.

The Truth About a Lie

by Tiffany Buckner- Kameni

Copyright

United States Copyright Office

© 2014, The Truth About a Lie
Tiffany Buckner- Kameni
info@tiffanykameni.com

ISBN-13: 978-0615974903

ISBN-10: 0615974902

Dedication

I dedicate this book to the one and only
YAHWEH. You are the head of my life; the
very breath of my soul, and I love You with my
whole heart.

Table of Contents

Introduction..IX

What is a Lie?...1

The Effects of Lying................................23

Why Do We Lie?....................................35

Layers of Lies.......................................47

Infected With Lies..................................55

How Lies Destroy Communities........................63

How Lies Destroy Marriages............................75

A Liar's Fast...87

How to Stop Lying...................................91

Learning to Tell the Truth................................107

The Pride Detector Test...............................115

The Great I AM and You...................................137

Largely Ignored Truths................................145

Spotting a Liar..155

10 Scriptures About Lying.............................161

Introduction

What's in a lie? Most of us want to know.
Truthfully, we've been raised and taught to lie
more than we were taught to be truthful. We
have learned to lie, and we have learned to
dismiss lies as harmless tales that we speak
for our own good. But that's not the truth. Lies
kill people; lies destroy lives, and lies ruin
GOD'S plans for us in the realm of the earth.

For every lie told, something dark is released
into our hearts, lives and relationships. Let's
face it: A lie can never do good to anyone or
for anyone.

In The Truth About a Lie, we are going to
dissect what a lie is and what a lie does.
Without knowledge or understanding, we'll
often repeat the patterns that enslave us,
but once we know better; we'll do better.

What is a Lie?

How many times in a day do you tell a lie? There has been a lot of research behind lies, and the facts say that the average person lies between 8 to 56 times a day. If we're awake sixteen hours of the day, this means the average person lies between .5 and 3.5 times every hour. Why is it that we seem to lie by default?

The truth is, we are taught to lie by our parents or whomever has raised us. How so? We watched our parents lie to one another. We watched our parents lie on one another. We watched our parents refuse to take responsibility for their own actions. Then, we listened to our parents as they lied to us about the Easter Bunny, the Tooth Fairy and Santa Claus. We believed every word they told us. When we told a lie to our parents, we were often scolded or disciplined, and we were told that our actions were wrong. And then, that inevitable day came when we found out that our parents weren't always truthful with one another, and even worse than that, our parents weren't always truthful with us. At the same time, we watched movies full of lies; we had friends who seemed to benefit from their lies, and we had relatives who made a living out of telling lies. Therefore, to lie didn't seem like such a bad thing. At church, the pastor preached against lies, but as children, most of us weren't paying any attention to the pastor during church service; we were watching the clock. Telling lies became just another item on that infamous long list of things we were told not to do. Nevertheless, we discovered that it seemed almost impossible for us not to tell a lie. So what did we do? We learning how to lie with a straight face. We practiced looking our parents in the eyes while telling lies. There seemed to be a benefit to lying. After all, we'd gotten a few of our parents, teachers and friends to agree to giving us something we wanted just by telling lies. Lies became like fake money. In other words, we could benefit from those seemingly harmless words if only we could make them look and sound as real as possible.

Even though we were told not to lie, we were rarely told why we shouldn't lie. Sure, many of us listened to our parents tell us that telling lies were bad and GOD did not like it when we told lies, but truthfully, this isn't enough to make a person reconsider the way they think or speak. As human beings, we need an in-depth understanding of what we are participating in; otherwise, we will continue to do what we feel is right until it becomes a part of us. That's why most people default to lying. In a parent's attempt to teach their children not to lie, they only teach them to better conceal those lies because most adults don't understand what lies are and what lies do.

But just what is a lie? Many people could give you their versions of what a lie is, but they'd be telling you the same lies that they'd believed in their hearts. If asked what a lie is, the average person would tell you that a lie is anything that is not true. If asked what the truth is, the average person would tell you that the truth is basically a fact that's been tested and proven or it's one's reality, but this is a lie. How so? A fact and the truth are not one and the same. A fact is man's version of the truth, established by man's findings; nevertheless, a fact can be discredited, reviewed and re-established. That's the history of mankind. Anytime a scientist conducts research and establishes what he or she says is a fact, another scientist sets out to disprove that person's theory and to set another theory in motion. Therefore, one man's truth (in the realm of the earth) is another man's lie. All the same, the word "reality" comes from the word "real." One man's reality is not necessarily another man's reality. For example, let's say there are two men who live on the opposite sides of town. One man is wealthy and lives in a gated community. His neighborhood is safe; therefore, he oftentimes leaves his doors unlocked, just as most of his neighbors do. He trusts his neighbors so much so that he tells them when he's going to be out of town so they can watch his house. The other guy in this example is impoverished and lives in an urban area. His neighborhood is dangerous; therefore, he keeps his doors and windows locked at all times. He oftentimes does not trust his neighbor. As a matter of fact, if he's going out of town, or even just going to work, he will likely seek to hide this from his neighbor out of fear that his neighbor may break into his home. He may even go as far as leaving the lights and television on to ward off potential burglars.

If both men were given platforms to help establish laws, they would work in opposition of one another because their realities are different. The wealthy man may seek ways to help himself and others like him become wealthier. To him, life is easy and the poor man is just another lazy human being who wants a hand-out. The poor man many seek ways to better his community, establish more jobs and have pay increases for the people he could relate most to. To him, life is oftentimes difficult, and the rich man is just another unsympathetic and spoiled child who is blind to what's going on in this world. Which guy is telling the truth? In trying to establish what the truth is, most people elect lies as truth in their hearts, and that's

why there is such a divide in the United
States of America. Every man has his own
reality, and most people try to establish
their realities as truth.

But what is the truth? The Truth is more
than just a word; the Truth is the living
WORD of GOD. The Truth is whatever
GOD has spoken into existence. The Truth
is the actual power of GOD established by
GOD. The Truth cannot be discredited by
man, even though many have attempted to
challenge HIM. The Truth is the WORD
and the WORD is the Truth; therefore,
GOD is HIS WORD and HIS WORD is
Truth.

There are a couple of scriptures that will
shed light on the Truth, and this will better
help us understand who the Truth is.
John 1:1-5: "In the beginning was the
Word, and the Word was with God, and the
Word was God. The same was in the

beginning with God. All things were made by him; and without him was not any thing made that was made. In him was life; and the life was the light of men. And the light shineth in darkness; and the darkness comprehended it not."

John 1:14: "And the Word was made flesh, and dwelt among us, (and we beheld his glory, the glory as of the only begotten of the Father,) full of grace and truth."

John 14:5: "Jesus saith unto him, 'I am the way, the truth, and the life: no man cometh unto the Father, but by me.'"

Let's rightly divide the scriptures to get a better understanding.

John 1:1-5 tells us that in the beginning there was the WORD of GOD, and the WORD was with GOD, and the WORD and GOD are one and the same. With this, we understand that GOD is HIS WORD. In this scripture, we also learn that all things were made by HIM. In Genesis 1 (entire chapter), is the account of GOD creating the earth. Throughout Genesis 1, we can see that GOD created all things simply by speaking them into existence.

On the first day:

"And God said, 'Let there be light,' and there was light" (Genesis 1:3).

On the second day:

"And God said, 'Let there be a firmament in the midst of the waters, and let it divide the waters from the waters'" (Genesis 1:6).

On the third day:

"And God said, 'Let the waters under the heaven be gathered together unto one place, and let the dry land appear: and it was so'" (Genesis 1:9).

On the fourth day:

"And God said, 'Let there be lights in the firmament of the heaven to divide the day from the night; and let them be for signs, and for seasons, and for days, and years: And let them be for lights in the firmament of the heaven to give light upon the earth:

and it was so'" (Genesis 1:14-15).

On the fifth day:

"And God said, 'Let the waters bring forth abundantly the moving creature that hath life, and fowl that may fly above the earth in the open firmament of heaven'" (Genesis 1:20).

On the sixth day:

"And God said, 'Let the earth bring forth the living creature after his kind, cattle, and creeping thing, and beast of the earth after his kind': and it was so'" (Genesis 1:24).

"And God said, 'Let us make man in our image, after our likeness: and let them have dominion over the fish of the sea, and over the fowl of the air, and over the cattle, and over all the earth, and over every creeping thing that creepeth upon the earth'"(Genesis 1:26).

As we can see, GOD spoke the Truth every day, for everything that GOD said was and is, and will continue to be. That's why it is impossible for GOD to tell a lie. Anything GOD says is established from the moment HE says it.

Finally, in John 1:1-5, we read that in GOD was life and the life was the light of men. The light shined in darkness, but the darkness did not comprehend the light. What does this mean? Life is established only by GOD. In HIS mouth is life, but GOD chose to do something amazing with man. Instead of speaking man into existence, GOD said, "Let us make man in our image, after our likeness." HE then went on to form man out of something HE'D already created: dust. For the WORD says, "And the LORD God formed man of the dust of the ground, and breathed into his nostrils the breath of life; and man became a living soul" (Genesis 2:7). In other words, we were custom-made by GOD. And what about John 1:5, which states that the light shined in darkness, but the darkness did not comprehend the light? Walk into any dark room and turn the light on. Does the room remain dark once the light is on? No, because darkness and light are in opposition of one another; nevertheless, light overpowers darkness. Instead of the darkness covering the light in a room, the light exposes what's in the darkness. So when the lights come on, it is easier for us to see because we are creatures created with sight. Anytime the Bible references darkness, it is referencing evil. Evil opposes GOD and GOD exposes evil. GOD is the Truth; HE is the Light, but anything that works in opposition of HIM is darkness.

John 1:14 states that the WORD was made flesh, and HE lived among us. How is this? GOD foretold of the coming of JESUS CHRIST starting in Genesis 3, when HE was speaking to the serpent (Satan). Of course, we know that the serpent deceived

What is a Lie?

Eve by lying to her. Before GOD judged mankind for disobeying HIM, HE spoke judgment over the serpent. "And I will put enmity between thee and the woman, and between thy seed and her seed; it shall bruise thy head, and thou shalt bruise his heel" (Genesis 3:15). What is enmity? Dictionary.Reference.com defines enmity as: "a feeling or condition of hostility; hatred; ill will; animosity; antagonism." Merriam-Webster Online defines enmity as: "positive, active, and typically mutual hatred or ill will." To have enmity between us and the devil is to purposely walk in opposing directions. What GOD was saying to the enemy is that HE would forgive us for our sins. HE would send HIS Son into the earth to redeem mankind; nevertheless, there was still no hope for the devil. He would still spend an eternity in hell. CHRIST was and is our saving grace; HE is the gulf that GOD has placed between mankind and the kingdom of darkness.

What is a Lie?

When Satan deceived Eve, his goal was to have mankind condemned to hell alongside him and his angels. But hell was not created for man. Hell was created for Satan and his angels. "Then shall he say also unto them on the left hand, Depart from me, ye cursed, into everlasting fire, prepared for the devil and his angels" (Matthew 25:41).

John 14:5 is an account of CHRIST JESUS speaking. In John 14:5, CHRIST is telling us who HE is. HE is the way. HE is the Truth. HE is the life. In other words, CHRIST YESHUA (JESUS) is the living WORD of GOD; the manifestation of the promise. HE is the spoken WORD alive. **HE is the way.** In saying that HE is the way, the LORD is telling us that HE is who we ought to follow. HE is the WORD of GOD; the promise manifested, and we have to follow HIM to be reconciled with GOD. HE is the WORD of GOD. Most of us think of the WORD of GOD as just scriptures written in the Bible, but the WORD lives and is more than just words on a page; HE is the promise manifested! Just as we know we should follow the scriptures and do as GOD told us to do, we need to understand that CHRIST is the living WORD; therefore, we must follow HIM. HE is the only way back to GOD, for HE is the WORD made alive.

HE is the Truth. We know that it is impossible for GOD to tell a lie. Everything that GOD speaks is and will continue to be because GOD spoke it into existence. Every word spoken by GOD is established and cannot return to HIM void. So when JEHOVAH (YAHWEH) speaks, HIS words are established; therefore, they are truth. When JEHOVAH spoke HIS WORD into the womb of Mary, HIS WORD manifested in her. Mary conceived a WORD from GOD, and that child became the living WORD of GOD in the flesh. That child was and is the Truth, for HE is the WORD of GOD.

He is the life. The wages of sin is death; therefore, because of sin, man was the living dead. Before mankind came into the earth, Satan opposed GOD and was cast out of Heaven along with his angels, and GOD declared judgment upon them. Anyone who sinned against GOD was condemned to hell. Of course, mankind wasn't in the earth, but it is believed that Satan fell not long after earth was created, right before man was created. We know that he'd fallen before the existence of Adam and Eve (who were the first people in the earth), but there is no information about when he'd fell. What we do know is earth had been created when he fell. "And war broke out in heaven: Michael and his angels fought with the dragon; and the dragon and his angels fought, but they did not prevail, nor was a place found for them in heaven any longer. So the great dragon was cast out, that serpent of old, called the Devil and Satan, who deceives the whole world; he was cast to the earth, and his angels were cast out with him" (Revelation 12:7-9).

When GOD judged Satan and his angels, they were cast out of heaven. Satan was envious of man because GOD loved man, so he tempted Eve into sin. He knew that once she sinned against GOD, the already declared judgment of GOD would be upon her head. He also knew that she'd take the fruit to her husband and cause him to fall into sin as well. After Satan deceived Eve, he was hoping that he'd ruined GOD'S creation, but GOD said something to him that would leave him traumatized and hateful of mankind. GOD told him that HE would send a <u>way</u> back to Heaven to man; nevertheless, there would still be no hope for Satan and his angels. Even though sin caused man to be condemned to hell, GOD gave man another chance at life, and that chance came through CHRIST JESUS. HE is the life that GOD spoke of; the reconciling grace of GOD sent into the realm of the earth to be a bridge for mankind to cross over hell back into the loving arms of his CREATOR. HE is the way.

What's even more amazing is the fact that people who died before the death and resurrection of CHRIST JESUS were sent to hell because the way had not been paved for them yet. CHRIST had to shed HIS Blood, and HIS Blood is the sin offering for us. But even though they were in hell, they were not in torments; instead, they were in what the Bible refers to as a prison. They weren't in the fire. GOD placed a divide in hell; putting HIS enemies in the fire, but keeping HIS children safe as they waited on the coming of the LORD. How do we know this? Recall the story of

Lazarus and the rich man. Lazarus was a believer, but he was also a beggar. The rich man was obviously an unbeliever or a hypocrite. He had no compassion for Lazarus, even though he saw Lazarus sitting outside his gates every day. He didn't feed Lazarus, nor did he provide housing for him. The Bible tells us that both men died and went to hell.

Luke 16:22-26 reads, "And it came to pass, that the beggar died, and was carried by the angels into Abraham's bosom: the rich man also died, and was buried; And in hell he lift up his eyes, being in torments, and seeth Abraham afar off, and Lazarus in his bosom. And he cried and said, Father Abraham, have mercy on me, and send Lazarus, that he may dip the tip of his finger in water, and cool my tongue; for I am tormented in this flame. But Abraham said, 'Son, remember that thou in thy lifetime receivedst thy good things, and likewise Lazarus evil things: but now he is

comforted, and thou art tormented. And
beside all this, between us and you there is
a great gulf fixed: so that they which would
pass from hence to you cannot; neither can
they pass to us, that would come from
thence.'

In reading the scriptures, we understand
that even though both men were in hell,
they were not living in the same conditions.
One man was comforted while the other
man was tormented. There was a gulf or
divide there that separated the believer
from the non-believer. What's even more
amazing is Abraham was there, but we do
know that Abraham is no longer in hell. We
know this because CHRIST went to hell
and set the captives free from hell.
1 Peter 3:18-19: "For Christ also hath once
suffered for sins, the just for the unjust, that
he might bring us to God, being put to
death in the flesh, but quickened by the
Spirit: By which also he went and preached

unto the spirits in prison."
1 Peter 3:31: "He seeing this before spake of the resurrection of Christ, that his soul was not left in hell, neither his flesh did see corruption."

From what we've read, it's clear that the Truth is the WORD of GOD. The Truth is every word proclaimed by GOD. A "fact" is what man believes and has established as his truth in the realm of the earth, but man's facts are not truths. They are man's perceived realities until they realize something else. In man's quest to find the truth, they have uncovered facts; temporary findings that can be proved to the senses: sight, hearing, touch, taste or smell. But always remember that what smells good to one man is a stench to another man.

What exactly is a lie then? A lie is the doctrine of Satan. It is anything that opposes who GOD is and what GOD said.

What is a Lie?

When JESUS was questioned by the Jews
who did not believe HIM, HE said, "Ye are
of your father the devil, and the lusts of
your father ye will do. He was a murderer
from the beginning, and abode not in the
truth, because there is no truth in him.
When he speaketh a lie, he speaketh of his
own: for <u>he is a liar, and the father of it</u>"
(John 8:44)."

The Effects of Lying

Lies seem harmless; right? After all, once we tell a lie, we oftentimes see the results we want, and we say that they are good. We even have what we refer to as "white lies." A white lie is supposedly a harmless lie told for the sake of helping someone or soothing someone. The truth is, there is no such thing as a harmless lie because lies are the doctrine of Satan. All the same, in calling evil good, we place ourselves in line for judgment. "Woe unto them that call evil good, and good evil; that put darkness for light, and light for darkness; that put bitter for sweet, and sweet for bitter!" (Isaiah 5:20).

But what are the effects of lying? Of course, man has his findings, but they don't embody the whole truth.

Lies separate us from GOD. Satan is a liar, and because he opposes GOD, he was cast out of Heaven. Lies oppose GOD for GOD is HIS WORD and HIS WORD is Truth. Even though we worship HIM with our mouths, when we are full of lies, we worship HIM in vain, because we are not worshiping HIM in truth or from our hearts. "Wherefore the Lord said, 'Forasmuch as this people draw near me with their mouth, and with their lips do honour me, but have removed their heart far from me, and their fear toward me is taught by the precept of men'"(Isaiah 29:13).

Lies stop us from hearing GOD. When we are full of lies, we are living vessels carrying Satan's doctrine of death. Of course, GOD is not going to instruct a liar unless HE'S leading him back to the truth.

Lies stop us from being blessed by GOD. GOD blessed us to be a blessing, but when a lie is stored up on the inside of us, we become vessels carrying that lie around. Imagine countries at war. They would not hire vessels who deliver weapons to their enemies to deliver weapons to them as well. If the United States were at war with China, and Russia delivered weapons to the United States, China would consider Russia its enemy. Because of that, China would end all trade relations with Russia. GOD works in a similar way. When we are vessels of the enemy, we can't expect GOD to bless us on every side, seeing as it is that we are working against HIM.

Lies pervert our gifts from GOD.
Imagine having a neighbor who hates you. This neighbor has gone above and beyond to destroy your good name and ruin your life. But even though this neighbor hates

you, he is best friends with your spouse. You buy groceries for your house, only to discover that your spouse has taken some of the food and given it to the neighbor. How would you feel? You'd be hurt; you'd be angry, and you'd probably be at a lawyer's office filing for divorce. Why is that? Your spouse has aligned himself/ herself with your enemy; therefore, you don't trust your spouse. All the same, it's hurtful and upsetting that the person you loved and trusted took what you brought home and gave it to your enemy. This is what many people do with the gifts GOD has given them. Sure, GOD can use whomever HE wants to, and the gifts and calling are without repentance. We can be gifted and used by the devil, as we witness everyday on our television screens. Once a man is anointed by GOD, he will remain anointed, even if he decides not to serve the LORD with his gifts. All the same, he will be punished for choosing to serve the enemy rather than choosing to serve GOD.

Lies grieve the HOLY SPIRIT. "Let no corrupt communication proceed out of your mouth, but that which is good to the use of edifying, that it may minister grace unto the hearers. And grieve not the Holy Spirit of God, whereby ye are sealed unto the day of redemption" (Ephesians 4:9-30).

Lies blind and pervert us to follow death. The LORD specifically told us that HE is the way, the Truth and the life. In doing so, HE was telling us the difference between HIM and our enemy. GOD leads us; Satan misleads us. GOD is the Truth, but Satan is the author of a lie. GOD is life, but Satan's doctrine leads to death. When we are blinded by lies, we can't see the light to follow the truth.

- "For the wages of sin is death; but the gift of God is eternal life through Jesus Christ our Lord" (Romans

6:23).

- "If we say that we have fellowship
with him, and walk in darkness, we
lie, and do not the truth: But if we
walk in the light, as he is in the light,
we have fellowship one with another,
and the blood of Jesus Christ his Son
cleanseth us from all sin" (1 John
1:6-7).

**Lies wage war against us from within
us.** Let's face it: We were designed by the
Truth for the Truth. We were not designed
to carry lies. It's just like putting diesel in a
gasoline vehicle. The vehicle was
designed to run on gas; therefore, if
someone was to put diesel in the engine
instead, the vehicle would not run.
Because we are loved by GOD and lies
come from the enemy of GOD, lies won't
work with us; they will work against us. A
lie perverts a man and causes him to self-
destruct because Satan designed lies for

the sole purpose of destroying mankind.

Lies wage war against a man's sanity.
Whatever a man believes, he receives. To believe something is to give it permission to enter into our hearts. Our hearts are our belief systems; therefore, anything that enters our hearts will affect the way we see, think and feel. When a lie enters a man, it begins to wage war against the Truth from within that man. In doing so, the person becomes double-minded, and eventually, many become unbelievers. To be double-minded means that the person is confused and does not know what or who to believe. This makes the person spiritually insane and unstable.

- "For the time will come when they will not endure sound doctrine; but after their own lusts shall they heap to themselves teachers, having itching ears; And they shall turn away their ears from the truth, and shall be turned unto fables" (2 Timothy 4:3-4).

- "A double minded man is unstable in all his ways" (James 1:8).
- "O foolish Galatians, who hath bewitched you, that ye should not obey the truth, before whose eyes Jesus Christ hath been evidently set forth, crucified among you?" (Galatians 3:1)

Of course, once the man makes up his mind as to who and what he believes, he is then settled as a believer or a non-believer.

Lies cause us to deceive others. When we believe lies, we tell lies. Just as Eve took the fruit to Adam and caused him to yield to sin, lies are carried by anyone who has believed them, and often delivered to the people closest to them. In delivering those lies, we become mouthpieces for the serpent, and we cause our brethren to fall.

Lies affect our parenting. GOD is our

FATHER and HE speaks the Truth at all times. When we become fathers and mothers, we are supposed to lead our children back to GOD, but how can this be done if we are being misled by the doctrine of Satan? Many people take their children to church, read the Bible with them often, but lead them in the way of sin. They are double-minded parents who confuse their children because they too are confused. Somehow, they have come to believe that sin is harmless; therefore, they pursue their own lusts, all the while coming to church. One thing about confusion is it takes our peace from us and causes us to walk in darkness.

- "For God is not the author of confusion, but of peace, as in all churches of the saints" (1 Corinthians 14:33).
- "But whoso shall offend one of these little ones which believe in me, it were better for him that a millstone

were hanged about his neck, and
that he were drowned in the depth of
the sea" (Matthew 18:6).

Lies affect our health. Do you truly
believe that something designed against
mankind would work for mankind? No.
Lies invite death into our bodies. For
example, if a person is told they have
cancer and they believe it, they will receive
it. But if a person believes what the WORD
says about the believer and his portion,
they will receive their portion of GOD'S
blessings.

- "For the wages of sin is death; but
  the gift of God is eternal life through
  Jesus Christ our Lord" (Romans
  6:23).
- "If my people, which are called by my
  name, shall humble themselves, and
  pray, and seek my face, and turn
  from their wicked ways; then will I
  hear from heaven, and will forgive

their sin, and will heal their land" (2 Chronicles 7:14).

Lies affect our perception of life and others. Just like lies blind us, lies also affect the way we perceive others and the way we perceive life. When we have been deceived by lies, we often believe whatever evil our hearts regurgitate. We begin to see evil as good and good as evil. At the same time, we wrongly judge others because our perception has been our deception.

Lies cause us not to believe GOD. At any given time, GOD is speaking to us. HE loves us and wants to protect us, but when we are full of lies, we have trouble believing HIM. Because of this, we become reckless and put ourselves in harm's way daily. All the same, when we don't believe GOD, we won't receive HIM in our hearts. If we don't receive HIM, it is because we have received HIS enemy and HIS enemy's doctrine.

Lies affect our worship, and causes our worship to become unacceptable to GOD. "God is a Spirit: and they that worship him must worship him in spirit and in truth" (John 4:24).

There are many things that lies do to us, but one thing that lies do not do for us is to bless us. Anytime a lie comes forward, it comes as a curse. Sure, a lie may come covered in beautiful attire, and drenched in a pleasant aroma, but when we walk in light, we can truly see the hideousness of the lie, and we can smell its stench.

Why Do We Lie?

As mentioned earlier, the "facts" say that the average person lies 8-56 times a day. Again, what is established as a fact is not necessarily truth because another person will come along and seek to discredit the established fact in order to establish a new one. Nevertheless, the truth is we oftentimes lie, but for every man, the amount of times we lie in a day differs. At the same time, our reasons for lying also varies from person to person.

Most people lie out of ignorance. They speak what they believe to be truth or what they are unsure of. Some of the most common reasons for lying include, but are not limited to: ignorance, pride, fear and rebellion.

<u>Ignorance</u>

Many people simply don't know the truth; therefore, they speak what has manifested itself as their realities. Ignorance doesn't mean that one is stupid; it simply means that the truth is available, but they are ignoring it. Ignorance's root word is "ignore." It means that the information is present for the taking; nevertheless, the person has chosen to ignore it. For example, most of us have the WORD of GOD available to us. We have Bibles; we know believers, and we have the Internet. Howbeit, many believers choose not to read their Bibles often or even seek the WORD of GOD in its entirety. They instead choose to read the Bible on Sunday morning while in church service. Then again, many who read the Bible don't meditate on the WORD. Instead, they read the words as they are lined up on the pages of the Bible, not taking a moment to consider what the words mean. We learned to read, but not comprehend and this isn't enough.

Pride

Let's say you were dealing with a person who likes to come off as knowledgeable, and you present a question to them that they don't know the answer to. Because of pride, they feel obligated to give you an answer, rather than confessing that they don't know the answer. In giving you an answer, they spill lies, and you are given the opportunity to receive what they've said or reject it. To receive it is to believe it, and if you believe it, it enters your heart and becomes a part of your belief system. Pride is one of the most common reasons for believers to lie, along with ignorance. Why is that? Because many of us present ourselves as being at a particular place in our walks, and we feel that not knowing the answer to certain questions or not knowing how to approach certain situations shows us in a bad light. But we have to remember to approach a question and a situation without an answer so that GOD can answer through us. It is not our knowledge that will always come from our lips. In speaking the WORD to others, we will oftentimes discover new knowledge as GOD pours into us and we pour out onto others. Nevertheless, many people are hindered by pride; therefore, they are puffed up and can't hear from Heaven. "These six things doth the LORD hate: yea, seven are an abomination unto him: A proud look, a lying tongue, and hands that shed innocent blood, An heart that deviseth wicked imaginations, feet that be swift in running to mischief, A false witness that speaketh lies, and he that soweth discord among brethren" (Proverbs 6:16-19).

<u>Fear</u>
Oftentimes, a man will tell a lie because he fears the consequences. We know that

there are consequences for our actions,
and sometimes, we don't want to face
them. For those of us who were disciplined
as children, we learned to lie to avoid being
disciplined. Some of our parents spanked
us; some of our parents beat us, and some
of our parents punished us by taking things
or privileges away from us. So, as children
and teens, we learned to perfect the art of
lying. We felt that our parents did not
understand the times; therefore, they were
being overly dramatic about our choices.
As adults, we oftentimes think the same
way. We fear that our bosses may magnify
situations we consider to be minor
incidents. We fear that our spouses may
overreact and read more into our decisions.
We fear that our children may take the
wrong roads, so we lie. Nevertheless, a lie
is never harmless and will always do more
harm than good. The truth may hurt
someone's feeling for a short time, but they
have the rest of their lives to get over it and

accept it. A lie may please someone for a short time, but lies oftentimes reveal themselves in layers, and each revelation hurts the person who received the lie. It hurts them over a period of time as the lie continues to unfold, revealing more and more of the truth.

<u>Rebellion</u>

Rebellion is man's way of saying that he refuses to do as GOD commanded because he feels that doing otherwise would benefit him more. It goes without saying, many believers rebel against the LORD every day because many believers have the same thinking patterns as people in the world. They see ways to advance, and in order to step forward into what they perceive as elevation, they purposely tell lies. This happens on and off the job scene, but the truth is elevation comes only from GOD. Man gives us ranks, titles and raises in the realm of the earth, but this isn't elevation. Oftentimes, it's a snare. Anything that is not given by GOD stands on a shaky foundation and can be brought down by a slight revealing of the truth. 1 Corinthians 3:7 reads, "So then neither is he that planteth any thing, neither he that watereth; but God that giveth the increase." In this, GOD is telling us that HE is the One who increases us and all that we have. But because many have believed upon the lies they were told, they have chosen to rebel against the truth for the sake of personal gain. Everything GOD designed is designed to benefit HIS people as a whole, and anytime a person spends too much time loving on themselves and not on their neighbors, they will become self-absorbed and sin against GOD. They will establish themselves as their own gods; oftentimes, not recognizing that they've done so. They will follow after their own lusts and seek to advance themselves in the realm of the earth, not considering what their actions would do to others.

There are many types of liars, but they are all in opposition of GOD. The most infamous liar is the habitual liar. A habitual liar is a person who lies by default. They've become so comfortable with lying that lying is a part of most of their daily communications. They may speak a little truth and a whole lot of lies, and some speak a lot of truth with a few lies between the lines. In doing so, they become as the serpent; having a fork in their tongue. The fork in the serpent's tongue represents his double-mindedness and ability to speak truth as well as lies. The heart of a habitual liar is dark and full of false doctrine. Anytime a lie attempts to enter us, we become uncomfortable and we oftentimes consider the lie before receiving it…just as Eve considered the fruit before picking it. But a habitual liar will oftentimes not consider lies. Instead, they receive anything that makes sense to them or that promises to benefit them in some way. A habitual liar oftentimes lies for no reason other than lying is a habit to them.

There is a liar who lies for image preservation. He has established an identity for himself, and he seeks to maintain that identity. This, of course, is a liar who intentionally lies to alter man's perception of him. He is an especially rebellious and crafty liar because his lies are told because of selfish ambition.

Then there is the liar who told one lie to protect himself or his marriage. In doing so, he had to tell another lie to cover the first lie, and then another to cover that lie. After a while, he finds himself telling another lie every time the truth threatens to reveal his lies. One thing about lies is that they are unstable and will continue to peel away until the truth is revealed; therefore, a person who told one lie has to use more lies as an adhesive to keep the truth from being uncovered.

Another liar is the people's liar. An example is a lawyer, a politician or a person who is very protective of their friends. We all know that lawyers lie for a living and politicians lie for political and personal gain. But the most interesting of them all is the liar who purposely lies to protect others. Such liars are openly rebellious, crafty and unrepentant. Anytime a person is comfortable telling lies, it is because they believe the notion that some lies are harmless and that some lies are necessary.

But why tell a lie? Again most people who tell lies do so for varying reasons; nevertheless, many come to realize that it would have been better to tell the truth and accept the consequences than to conceal

the truth and destroy the very thing they
were trying to protect.

Layers of Lies

The truth is a whole, but a lie comes in parts. The truth is established and confirms itself again and again; whereas, a lie is not established and can only stay afloat when believed. Anytime we speak the truth, we are speaking what GOD has already established; therefore, in searching out our words, the person we spoke to will only find confirmation. Anytime we speak lies, we are speaking the doctrine of Satan; therefore, in searching out our words, the person we spoke to will either find out that we are liars or they'll find us covering the original lie with another lie. In order for a lie to stand, it has to be constantly built on when challenged.

Because one man would fold under

pressure easily, the enemy has established many liars who believe certain lies. He then gives them a title to separate them from others. This title distinguishes their doctrine from other doctrines. The purpose of doing this is to war against the truth in numbers. A largely believed doctrine continues to grow because of the many people who believe it. Each person who believes it adds to the strength of that doctrine; nevertheless, it takes one truth to destroy an army of lies. Each person who believes in that doctrine becomes a layer of that doctrine. The doctrine has the appearance of truth because it is largely guarded, but it has no foundation and no substance. Such doctrines include, but are not limited to Atheism, Agnosticism, Scientology and Free-thought.

Atheism is the belief that there is no GOD or gods.

Agnosticism is the belief that one can neither prove or disprove the existence of

GOD. It is to be unsure, double-minded and oftentimes is the prelude to Atheism. Scientology is basically free-thinking or the belief that all things exist through nature. It is to erect science as a god. Scientology serves the belief that there is no sin. Free-thinking is the belief that one can believe what they want to believe. Free thinkers often reject religion and GOD. Atheism, Agnosticism and Scientology are all rooted in free-thinking.

As you can see, the foundation of these cults is to be free from the WORD of GOD. Satan created layers to the lies so that any person who was unsure of what to believe could find these same foundations in every cult that is against GOD, but see Christianity as an imprisoned way of thinking. To do this, the enemy led man to establish many false and imprisoning religions that oppress people. He then sent many false teachers into the Christian faith in an attempt to discredit Christianity. Once he established these false teachers, he took them up the ranks amongst believers and then brought them down publicly. He exposed their darkness: greed, lust, perversions, blasphemies and lies. After that, he continued to send out false teachers who did not claim Christianity, but claimed that Christianity was an enslaving religion full of hypocrites and religious dogma. Finally, he established facts as truth amongst men. He gave those facts the appearance of truth, and told man that those facts would stand against Christian doctrine. But there was a problem. His lies kept falling apart layer by layer; therefore, he had to send out another liar to establish another lie as man's version of the truth. To stop the truth from advancing amongst men, the enemy established many lying institutions with the purpose of confusing them. "Another parable put he forth unto them, saying, ' The kingdom of heaven is likened unto a man which sowed good seed in his field: But while men slept, his enemy came and sowed tares among the wheat, and went his way. But when the blade was sprung up, and brought forth fruit, then appeared the tares also. So the servants of the householder came and said unto him, Sir, didst not thou sow good seed in thy field? from whence then hath it tares? He said unto them, An enemy hath done this. The servants said unto him, Wilt thou then that we go and gather them up? But he said, Nay; lest while ye gather up the tares, ye root up also the wheat with them. Let both grow together until the harvest: and in the time of harvest I will say to the reapers, Gather ye together first the tares, and bind them in bundles to burn them: but gather the wheat into my barn'" (Matthew 13:24-30).

What are the tares? The tares are Satan's children who live amongst GOD'S children with the intent of deceiving them, and causing them to fall. As witnessed in this modern-day, there are many tares amongst the elect, and they are full of many unsound doctrines. In addition to being full of lies, they are oftentimes very vocal about what they believe, taking to politics and coming against Christianity with force. There is one Truth, but there are many lies, just as there are many liars.

Another way lies occur in layers is through our personal relationships. Anytime we tell a lie to someone, that lie begins to contend with the truth in them. If they believe the lie into their hearts, it begins to affect the way they think and their perception. Nevertheless, the truth will continue to stand and wage war against the lies that are in that person. In order for that lie to stand, the liar must continue to build upon that lie with more lies. When the truth finally begins to cause each lie to retreat,

the people who believed the lies has to
have their hearts broken while the lies
attempt to exit their hearts. When they
have learned to love those lies, they will
often pursue the lies because a broken
heart oftentimes feels unbearable, but a lie
can be comforting for a while. That's why
you'll find that woman who has trouble
letting go of an enemy who has
camouflaged herself as a friend for years.
Letting go of the friend isn't oftentimes the
strongman that keeps her in that friendship.
Letting go of the lies is what she fears.
Once she believes the truth in, she will
happily distance herself from that friend.
But why does she choose to keep the lies
when the truth is standing in plain view?
Because the truth has to break her heart in
order to enter it. The lies that were in her
must be challenged, overcome and then
rejected. Once the truth comes in, the
mystery of her friendship begins to unveil
itself. Suddenly, every lie she was told

begins to surface, break her heart and evaporate. After a while, every new revelation is no longer painful to her because she has now opened her heart up for the truth.

Every lie has to be built upon, but the truth tears down anything that is not of GOD. How can you tell when you've been lied to? Anytime a person has to give you new information to stabilize the old information they gave you, they are telling lies. When a person speaks the truth, the truth will remain consistent and unmoving.

Infected With Lies

Lies are infectious. Anytime a lie is received by one person, it is then carried by that person to countless others. Once those lies have been believed in, they begin to wage war against that person's thinking patterns. It causes the person to question themselves and every truth they've believed. Like a disease, lies infect a man by coming against the way he was created. We were never created to hold lies; we were created by the Truth for the Truth; therefore, we cannot properly process lies.

Think about processed food. Our bodies cannot properly digest processed foods, and when we take them in, they do more harm to our bodies than good. Our bodies are able to extract a few nutrients from these foods, but the only benefits to these foods are that they are filling. They remove the hunger, and we are able to survive on them. That's how lies work. Our souls cannot properly process lies, and when we take them in, they do more harm to us than good. We are able to extract a few truths from the lies we are told, but the only benefits to those lies are that they give us answers where there were questions. In other words, where we were hungry for an answer, we are filled with an answer. Even though those answers are lies, they are filling to our soul. After we've been satisfied with lies, and we are able to move about without obvious constraint, we carry those filling lies to others who are hungry, and many of them receive the lies.

As a lie begins to unpack itself in one's heart, it first has to evict anything that has been believed in. It's coming in to take the place of other beliefs, and cause us to question any truths that audition for a role in our hearts. A lie first has to cause the man to become double-minded because it's not easy for any of us to reject what we believe, so we'll question the truth while questioning the lie. We try to reason within ourselves as to which report we ought to receive in our hearts, and this causes us to become unstable. Most people walk in instability for years because they aren't sure which report they want to accept as truth for their lives. After a while, people can become comfortable with being unstable. An unstable person will surround himself or herself with others who are unstable. This helps them to feel "normal" and to stop questioning themselves.

Once a lie has been believed into the heart, it then causes the man to self-destruct. After all, man was not created to survive only on food. Man needs the WORD to survive; otherwise, he becomes the walking dead. "But he answered and said, It is written, 'Man shall not live by bread alone, but by every word that proceedeth out of the mouth of God'" (Matthew 4:4).

A person full of lies is not a person who has peace because every lie that they have believed upon is shaken up and destroyed by the truth. Every lie is peeled back, only to reveal another lie until the whole truth is uncovered. A liar has to tell themselves lies to get by. They begin to do the work of the enemy for him in their own hearts because living a lie has become their normal. They continue to consider many new facts or false doctrines in an attempt to silence the truth from within. Everything that makes sense to them is believed by them as they attempt to find their way in life. This causes them to be led by evil, enchanted by lies and given to the enemy. "Trust in the LORD with all thine heart; and lean not unto thine own understanding. In all thy ways acknowledge him, and he shall direct thy paths. Be not wise in thine own eyes: fear the LORD, and depart from evil." (Proverbs 3:5-7).

A person who is full of lies is oftentimes full of rage because the war from within has caused them to become warriors who aren't sure which army to ally themselves with. Some become meek liars who appear to be harmless, but within them, there is a war going on, and they continue to become more and more unstable by the minute. Others become vocal liars who appear to be trustworthy because they openly pour out the wicked contents of their hearts for everyone to see. Some become contentious liars who make it their own personal missions to enter into every debate where the truth is present.

Once a lie has entered a man's heart, it

slowly begins to open the man up for death. We have to understand that death is Satan's will for us, but it is the will of GOD that we live and declare the works of the LORD. Satan knows that the wages of sin is death, so he entices a man to sin. "Then when lust hath conceived, it bringeth forth sin: and sin, when it is finished, bringeth forth death" (James 1:15). In other words, lies are terminal and infectious, and that's why the enemy sets out to recruit liars to spread his venomous doctrine.

The only cure for lies and liars is the Truth. There is no other way. GOD'S WORD must be believed to be received by us, and HIS WORD will evict all false doctrine and begin to heal us. But when a person has received countless lies, they seek healing (something that is already provisioned for the believer) in man's doctrines. Man cannot cure a disease; he can only trim the hedges of what grows from the lies that are within. Some people believe that they are cured because certain ailments never manifest in their health again, but oftentimes, another ailment branches off from what they've allowed to root within their hearts. If you want to cure the man, you must give him the healing balm of GOD'S WORD, and he must self-medicate himself with the WORD until it becomes his truth. Once lies are evicted from our hearts, it is then and only then that we can live in the blessings that GOD has provisioned for the believer.

How Lies Destroy Communities

Have you ever noticed how different two neighboring communities can be from one another? One community is safe and the people who reside in it are prosperous and settled. Another community is dangerous and the people who reside in it are impoverished and some of them are unstable. What type of divide occurred between these two communities to cause such a huge difference in the two? It's simple. Lies are oftentimes the divides that separate people from one another.

If you are a part of working class America, you likely are against laziness and people getting free and undeserved money. You are also likely against rich people getting tax cuts. You've learned the value of working for what you have, and you believe that if every American was to do as you are doing, this place would be a better place to live. And you are right…somewhat. In order to improve a community, the heads or leaders of that community must be righteous; otherwise, they will cause the members of that community to fall. "When the righteous are in authority, the people rejoice: but when the wicked beareth rule, the people mourn" (Proverbs 29:2).

But the enemy in his craftiness has given us the choice of electing a Democrat or a Republican. The candidates that are oftentimes presented to the people are self-absorbed and power thirsty. Getting elected into office is just something else for them to add to their growing portfolios. The people are not their concerns. In choosing, the people oftentimes try to elect the candidate who appears to be the lesser of two evils. In a sense, it's like being handed a ballot with a devil running for office against a principality. Voters oftentimes choose the devil because he appears to have more hope for change than his opponent.

When that devil takes office, what does he do? He begins to contend with the WORD for the sake of personal gain. He then elects a principality to serve on the board with him. The truth is, you can't have evil in leadership and look for something good to happen…unless that leader is overturned and his power stripped from him. Anyone who contends with the WORD and causes the people to fall is evil…period! Nevertheless, the communities fall because of the leadership of those communities. That's why the LORD tells us not to involve ourselves with the world. The world is HIS enemy. GOD does not want the believers to be under worldly leadership. HE has given us leaders after HIS own heart. "And

I will give you pastors according to mine heart, which shall feed you with knowledge and understanding" (Jeremiah 3:15).

When a liar takes office, he spreads the venom of his lies amongst the people. The people then become corrupt, and selfishness begins to become each man's personal doctrine. Believers who participate in this masquerade will begin to side with one of the evils and will contend with the truth and anyone bearing the truth. That's why you'll hear so many self-proclaimed Christians saying things like, "Judge ye not unless ye be judged." Sure, GOD tells us not to judge one another, but to judge someone and rebuke someone is not the same, as most people believe. If one says to an adulteress that she was wrong and GOD will punish her for her sin, they have not judged her; they have rebuked her. To rebuke means to correct or to chasten with words. To judge her is to throw her in prison or to sentence her to death. When the woman was found in adultery, and the men brought her before CHRIST, they wanted to see what HE would say. HE said to them that the man who was without sin was to be the one who threw the first stone. There was no man present who was without sin; therefore, they dropped their stones and walked away. The sin was not in them saying that she was found in adultery, because she was. The sin was not in them saying that what she'd done was wrong and against GOD, because it was. The sin was them deciding upon themselves to play GOD. They wanted to take her life for what she'd done, and this was judgment. When a believer rebukes another believer for something they've done, they are doing their parts as believers. "Reprove not a scorner, lest he hate thee: rebuke a wise man, and he will love thee" (Proverbs 9:8). The problem is rebuking an unbeliever.

The world will do as the world is led by Satan to do, but the believer is to uphold the WORD of GOD in their lives. They are to take up their crosses and follow the LORD; nonetheless, many pick up flags and follow the perverted leaders of this world. Many pledge allegiance to a man-made flag, not understanding that we can never ally ourselves with this world or anything of it. "For the rod of the wicked shall not rest upon the lot of the righteous; lest the righteous put forth their hands unto iniquity" (Psalm 125:3).

When a wicked man is in leadership, he opens the door of opportunity for other wicked men to come into leadership. After all, we seek others who are like us. A wicked man does not want to work with a righteous man; he wants people who are like him to serve with him. "Can two walk together, except they are agreed?" (Amos 3:3).

In that case, should a believer participate in the electing of political figures? We'll let the scriptures answer that for us, since this is a highly debatable question.

Proverbs 29:16: "When the wicked are multiplied, transgression increaseth: but the righteous shall see their fall."

Note: Many who read this will decide that voting for political figures is good because it allows them to keep the wicked out of office. The truth is the world's system was designed for the world and will not impact a believer who has separate himself or herself from it. How can we keep a wicked man out of office when we are only presented with evil candidates. Let the world handle its own. The wicked are multiplied nowadays because many believers have allied themselves with the world.

Psalm 26:4: "I have not sat with vain persons, neither will I go in with dissemblers. I have hated the congregation of evil doers; and will not sit with the wicked. I will wash mine hands in innocency: so will I compass thine altar, O LORD."

Note: We know that David was a man after GOD'S own heart, and here he is saying that he did not and would not sit in the congregation of the unrighteous. He says he would wash his hands in innocency; meaning that he is not involving himself in the world or the world's practices.

Psalms 1:1-1:2: "Blessed is the man that walketh not in the counsel of the ungodly, nor standeth in the way of sinners, nor sitteth in the seat of the scornful. But his delight is in the law of the LORD; and in his law doth he meditate day and night."

Note: Many say, "Where are my blessings? I have prayed; I have fasted, and I have sought the LORD for answers, but my blessings seem to avoid me." But GOD told us where the blessings are. HE said that "blessed" is the man who <u>does not</u> walk in the counsel of the ungodly; blessed is the man who <u>does not</u> stand in the way with sinners, and blessed is the man who <u>does not</u> sit in the seat of the scornful. On average, how many believers actually separate themselves in this manner? Many participate in the world and the world's events; nevertheless, they justify their choices with the lies they have come to believe.

James 4:4: "Ye adulterers and adulteresses, know ye not that the friendship of the world is enmity with God? Whosoever therefore will be a friend of the world is the enemy of God."
Note: Why does the LORD refer to those who are friends of the world as adulterers and adulteresses? For the same reason HE refers to HIMSELF as our husbands. Imagine that you are married and you

found out that your spouse was hanging out with his or her ex. They've been going to dinner together, arguing with one another, holding hands and they may have even entered into one another's bedrooms. How would you feel? What if they'd never had sex? Would you still feel betrayed? Of course you would! After all, that's your spouse and what they've committed (if no sex was involved) was emotional adultery. It's simple. We can't hang out with the world, knowing that the world is against GOD, and then come home and smooth things over with the LORD.

John 15:19: "If ye were of the world, the world would love his own: but because ye are not of the world, but I have chosen you out of the world, therefore the world hateth you."

Note: This is the part that most believers don't understand. The world does not love us; it hates us. Therefore, it is not wise to involve yourself in the world or its practices.

But some would say, "Well, I've been voting for years because I want to make sure that the wrong person doesn't get into office." That's like saying you've been going to the house of a witch looking for a spell to drive another witch out of town. You simply cannot cure evil with evil. All the same, the world will worry about its own, and GOD will always take care of HIS own. GOD will overthrow evil, but when the church aligns itself with the world, the church becomes a part of the world. There are many people who go to church, read their Bibles, and proclaim the LORD as their SAVIOR; all the while, participating in the world. "No man can serve two masters: for either he will hate the one, and love the other; or else he will hold to the one, and despise the other" (John 15:19).
Now, if you want to vote, that's totally up to you, but you should seek direction from

GOD before making a commitment either way.

To clean up our communities, the church has to get back in the position of leadership. GOD never intended for the world to have dominion over the church. The people of GOD has to come together and reject the lies they were told, and put the power back in the hands of the men and women who were elected by GOD to carry that power. Until then, evil will continue to lead those who walk in darkness, and they will continue to mislead GOD'S people.

How Lies Destroy Marriages

If you've ever been married, you would know how lies attack the institution of marriage. In marriage, we oftentimes tell lies with the intent of saving our marriages. After we believe we know our spouses and their limitations, we work hard not to cross those limits with them, and if we feel that we have went overboard, we attempt to cover up our errors with lies. In marriage, a liar oftentimes becomes defensive when his or her lies are questioned. The closer one gets to uncovering a liar's lie, the more abrasive the liar may become.

Pay attention to how dogs are. If a dog buries a bone in a certain area, he will begin to guard that area. Another dog may simply wander into that area, not knowing that a bone has been hidden there. Because of his intrusion, the wandering dog will likely be attacked by the guarding dog. Of course, the wanderer has no clue as to why he's being attacked. He only knows that he must defend himself and try to get away from his attacker. We do the same thing in marriage when we've told lies. The closer our spouses get to those lies, the more we attack them with words. Because they are getting closer and closer to uncovering the truth, we oftentimes begin to resent them. Why is this? Many of us do not understand that we are the ones who attacked our marriages by bringing lies into it, so we project the blame onto our spouses. In our minds, they are the ones putting the marriage in danger. They are the ones who won't let an issue go that we feel isn't that important. It was just a little lie, right? Of course not!

To get a better understanding of how lies

affect marriages, we must first understand how lies affect the individuals in marriages. We'll go with the notion that you are a man, and you've committed adultery against your wife. You've told her many lies to cover up your adultery because you don't want to lose her. Here's what happening to her. GOD is in her; therefore, she is a woman full of the Truth, but you are in her heart as well, and you are dropping off lies in a place that she trusted you to enter. The LORD told us to guard our hearts, for out of it flows the issues of life. She guarded her heart, but she let you in, and now, you're littering her heart with lies. She believes those lies because she loves you and does not want to lose her marriage. She does not want to believe that it is possible for you to commit adultery against her, so she believes the lies you've told. But something keeps happening to her when she gets some time alone. The Truth continues to challenge the lies you've told her, and she becomes double-minded. She comes to you again because the Truth has brought some things to her attention. She questions you again, and you tell another lie to cover up the lie that has begun to peel. She goes away and the Truth contends with the lie once again. She wasn't designed to receive a lie, and GOD does not want her to be double-minded. HE wants us full of the Truth at all times; therefore, in contending with the lies you've told her, HE isn't trying to destroy your marriage; HE is trying to keep HIS spot in her heart. HE knows that HE can fix your marriage if you only repent, but HE'S not willing to lose her to lies. She goes away again and the Truth continues to break her heart and challenge each lie. Now, her peace is disturbed because she's now double-minded. She cries and becomes even more unstable. She's now conducting her own investigation into what you are doing or what you have done. The problem isn't that she wants to fight with you; the problem is she's lost her peace, and she's now seeking the Truth so she could get back to that place of peace. In her attempt to find peace, she will come to you in many emotions. She will approach you with anger; she will come to you in pain; she will come to you in meekness, and she will come to you in the name of the LORD. She's not begging for a fight; she's begging to be restored to her peaceful place. She's begging to be reconciled with the Truth. After the Truth has been spoken to her, you will likely find her in a relaxed state of mind. Even though the truth was painful to her, she knows that she can work with you towards healing, and you'll likely not repeat the sin if you were willing to confess it. That's why GOD told us to confess our sins one to another. The whole time that you were lying to her, she had trouble believing GOD. You became a hindrance to her relationship with the FATHER because she had the GOD she loved telling her one thing and the husband she loved telling her another. You made her choose between you and HIM. She would believe GOD, but she has learned that she can be wrong as well; therefore, she begins to silence GOD'S voice because your lies are telling her that the voice is coming from a dark place in her heart. Your lies are leading her to believe that there is something wrong with her because she's accusing an innocent man of committing a treacherous act. Since she's become double-minded, the pain in her heart will intensify because the lies will attempt to escape her, but she will keep holding on to them because she wants to hold on to your words. The best thing to do is tell her the truth and accept the consequences. The consequences are not there to destroy you; they are there to chasten and teach you.

When we choose a spouse for ourselves,

what we are doing is asking them to open up their hearts to us. The heart is the central part of a man; a place where his beliefs are stored, and a place that GOD inhabits. In order for us to get into a relationship with that person, and to gain access to their hearts, we open up and show them the content of our hearts. When we attempt to conceal what is in our hearts, we become liars, and we gain access to their hearts through deception. And that's when their problems begin. As time goes on, the Truth will continue to contend with every lie stored up in the believers. Why?

- **Lies oppose the Truth.** "Hold fast the form of sound words, which thou hast heard of me, in faith and love which is in Christ Jesus. That good thing which was committed unto thee keep by the Holy Ghost which dwelleth in us" (2 Timothy 13:14). GOD tells us to hold onto sound

words, for these words are from
GOD, and they give us access to
HIM.

- **The HOLY SPIRIT lives in us.**
"What? Know ye not that your body
is the temple of the Holy Ghost which
is in you, which ye have of God, and
ye are not your own? For ye are
bought with a price: therefore glorify
God in your body, and in your spirit,
which are God's" (1 Corinthians 6:19-
20). Since we are temples of the
HOLY SPIRIT, we must keep our
temples undefiled. Do you really
believe the Truth wants to be
roommates with lies?

- **CHRIST has set us free, but lies
bind and blind believers.** "If the
Son therefore shall make you free,
you shall be free indeed" (John 8:36).
In telling lies, we do the work of
Satan, and we place yokes upon the
necks of GOD'S children. In doing

so, we imprison them; whereas, CHRIST has paid the price for their freedom. Even though they may be fully grown individuals, they are still GOD'S children, and in lying to them, we cause them to stumble. "But whoso shall offend one of these little ones which believe in me, it were better for him that a millstone were hanged about his neck, and *that* he were drowned in the depth of the sea" (Matthew 18:6).

- **When we are full of lies, we don't think soberly because our perceptions have been altered by the lies we've accepted.** "Wherefore gird up the loins of your mind, be sober, and hope to the end for the grace that is to be brought unto you at the revelation of Jesus Christ" (1 Peter 1:13). Lies are like strong liquor; they alter our perceptions, and causes us to walk about in a blind stupor. GOD gave us a sound mind, but the enemy's desire is that we become double-minded, uncertain and intoxicated with lies.

- **Lies divide the house, but GOD is for unity.** "But he, knowing their thoughts, said unto them, 'Every kingdom divided against itself is brought to desolation; and a house divided against a house falleth'" (Luke 11:17). Anytime lies enter a home, it divides that home and eventually causes the destruction of the family unit.

So what should we do when we are married, and we have secrets that we fear could destroy our marriages? It's simple. You have to tell the truth to your spouse and accept the consequences. All the same, it is better to approach the LORD and ask HIM how you can reveal the truth to your spouse. You have to repent to HIM first, and ask HIM to protect and strengthen your marriage. Be willing to tell your spouse the whole truth, and if they should decide to leave you, let them leave, but you must remain repentant and apologetic. If they return to you, or if they stay with you, they have done so with a sound mind, and the two of you came overcome it all with the help of the LORD.

Lies also destroy the family as a whole, because any children in that marriage will be hurt by everything that transpires as a result of the lies told. All the same, the children learn to lie, and they lose respect for the parent who has been found to be a liar. Any division in the home will cause the family to split down the middle.

A Liar's Fast

We've heard of fasting from food, but we can also fast from lies. Anytime you find that you have trouble telling the truth, you need to take active measures to overthrow the lies that are in your heart. A great way to do this is to fast against telling lies. This unconventional method will teach you the importance of telling the truth, and help you get to the root of your lying.

What should you do?
1. Decide the length of your liar's fast. It is better to fast from lying for twenty-one days or more because compulsive lying is a stronghold. On average, it takes 17-21 days to break a habit. If you don't believe you can go that long without telling a lie, start

with a three to seven day fast against lying. In that time, commit to telling the truth, no matter how hard it seems.

2. Punish yourself anytime you tell a lie. It's not easy to break a habit, but what you have to do is get your own attention anytime you tell a lie. When lies have become a part of your norm, you will find that lies flow through you without effort. A great punishment would be for you to fine yourself a certain amount of money every time you tell a lie. Give that money to the person you've lied to, and make sure it's enough money to hurt your feelings. If it's something as small as a dollar, it'll only become a laughing matter, and you won't take your fast seriously. But if it you penalize yourself $20 or more, you'll likely get your own attention, and you'll work harder to watch your

words.

3. Anytime you are afraid to tell the truth, be quiet and go into another room. In that room, take a notebook and a pen, and begin to write down the truth. This will help you to acknowledge the truth, and it'll make it easier for you to tell the truth to whomever you've lied to.

If you decide to fast against lying, make sure you disassociate yourself from liars in that time period. Eventually, you will have to disassociate yourself from them altogether, but if you don't feel as if you are ready to let them go, at least stop talking with them while you are fasting.

Another unconventional, but helpful method is to write confession notes and place them in public mailboxes, shipped to a complete stranger with no name or return postage. Make sure your notes are clean and addressed to the adults of that household.

A Liar's Fast

If your notes contain sexually explicit information, it is better not do mail that information, but to confess it to a counselor or someone you can trust.

During your fast, attempt to rid yourself of every lie you have received as truth, as well as clean up the lies you once told to others. The more you do this, the more unburdened you will feel. After going for a while without lying, you will never want to return to being a liar again.

How to Stop Lying

Let's get one thing straight before we get started. It's almost impossible to stop lying because we oftentimes tell lies unknowingly, but it is possible through CHRIST. You will need to consult with the LORD, and you will need to actively and consciously pay attention to the words that come out of your mouth.

There are some people that we lie to the most. Identify who those people are to you. You'll notice that in lying, there are certain relatives or friends whom you've told the most lies to. Oftentimes, it's because these people present themselves a certain way, and we don't want them to perceive us as failures. However, most people who intentionally make others feel intimidated aren't living as good as they lead others to believe. And if they are living fabulous lives, you have to understand that they've paid a great price to get to where they are. Never allow jealousy or pride to cause you to stumble.

When you're accustomed to lying to certain people, it's often indicative of evil communication, and you will likely have to end your alliances with those people. In most cases, there is something in them that leads you to feel as if you need to sin to impress, intimidate or match them. That's why we have to be aware of who and what we're dealing with.

1 Corinthians 15:33: "Be not deceived: evil communications corrupt good manners."
Amos 3:3: "Can two walk together, except they be agreed?"
1 John 2:10: "He that loveth his brother

abideth in the light, and there is none occasion of stumbling in him."

Matthew 7:16: "Ye shall know them by their fruits. Do men gather grapes of thorns, or figs of thistles?"

First off, we have to identify why we lie, and why we tell the most lies to certain individuals. In identifying the reason, we will have identified the spirit behind or guarding those lies. "For we wrestle not against flesh and blood, but against principalities, against powers, against the rulers of the darkness of this world, against spiritual wickedness in high places" (Ephesians 6:12).

For example, let's say that a cousin of yours makes you feel as if you need to boast when they are around because they are always talking about what they have and what they've done. In their presence, you feel inadequate, and you feel the need to compete with them. What's the root issue here? It could be the cousin. The cousin maybe lying and intentionally intimidating you because they are led by a spirit of pride, a spirit of jealousy and a spirit of lying. In this case, you would need to distance yourself from that cousin, for this is the very reason you feel pulled on to lie when in their presence. Their devils are seducing you.

Another issue could be that they have done well, and are just being their normal selves and talking about it. Around their friends who happen to be as successful as they are, their communication isn't looked at as boasting; it's simply having a conversation. With you, however, it's seen as boasting because you can't relate to them. In this case, the root of the issue would be jealousy or envy on your part. Anytime we are enticed by a spirit, we will often respond with another spirit. If that's the issue, you would need to actively bind jealousy and envy. It is not wise to ask or expect that cousin to cease from talking about their success in your presence unless they are boasting, and you are SURE of this. Jealousy and envy will cause a person to believe another person is intentionally trying to boast, when in reality, human beings talk about their realities openly, but when our realities don't match theirs, we often separate ourselves from them.

One more issue could be that the cousin is intimidated by you; therefore, they remember every good thing that has happened for them over the course of their lives to avoid talking about the countless bad things that they've had to endure. Maybe you make them feel as if they have to lie in your presence.

Whatever the issue is, you have to get to the root of it and pull it up. Always remember that lies are doctrine, and you won't be able to stop reading from that doctrine until you've evicted it from your heart and replaced it with truth.

To identify the root cause of lying, we must peel back the layers of our lies and ask ourselves why we told those lies. One thing you'll find is that every lie rests on a foundation in your heart. Telling the truth only slaughters the lie, but if the foundation remains intact, you will continue to tell lies. "But he answered and said, Every plant, which my heavenly Father hath not planted, shall be rooted up" (Matthew 15:13).

To get to the foundation, you must go in reverse through each lie you've told, and ask yourself, "Why did I tell this lie? What was I looking to gain? What was I worried about?" When confronting yourself, one of the very first spirits you'll encounter is a haughty spirit. A haughty spirit causes us to become filled with pride. You'll know you're dealing with a haughty spirit when you start to feel somewhat agitated, and you have trouble telling yourself the truth. Oftentimes, you'll know what the truth is, but you'll feel the need to cover it with words. You'll try to justify the lie to keep the lie, and you'll hide the truth in your heart. Don't do this. Immediately bind up that haughty spirit and openly speak the truth. To overcome pride, you have to humble yourself. Just as lies are defeated by truth, a haughty spirit is defeated by humility. In pride, you will likely begin to reason with yourself. For example, you'll say to yourself, "Well, it's not that I'm jealous of her. She's just a little too prissy for me." In this communication with yourself, you have identified two spirits: a haughty spirit and a spirit of jealousy. Jealousy will never admit to being jealousy because it's guarded by pride, and we can never justify disliking another human being simply because they are different from us. In identifying the spirits, we must bind them up, rebuke them with the WORD and cast them away from us. To keep them away, we must tell the truth.

Proverbs 16:18: "Pride goeth before destruction, and an haughty spirit before a fall."

Numbers 5:14: "And the spirit of jealousy come upon him, and he be jealous of his wife, and she be defiled: or if the spirit of jealousy come upon him, and he be jealous of his wife, and she be not defiled...."

Again, when you have trouble speaking the truth, don't speak at all. Go somewhere to be alone with the LORD, and lay your burden upon HIM. You have to fight through how you feel.

Another stronghold that causes us to lie is unforgiveness. Unforgiveness isn't a demonic spirit; it is a stronghold because it is rooted in pride. Unforgiveness is simply a symptom of being inhabited by a haughty spirit. It is a mindset that is birthed when pride and lies mate with one another. In unforgiveness, we have to exalt ourselves in order to minimize another person. The haughty spirit will say to us that we didn't deserve what that person did to us or someone we love. The lying spirit will say that our pain and our failures are the result of what that person did. The lying spirit will say that you will never have rest until you've dealt with that person. When these two spirits begin to reason with our minds, they lead us away from loving our brother, and when we consider what they are saying, hatred begins to form. Just as Eve picked the fruit from the Tree of the Knowledge of Good and Evil, we can pick love from the trees that GOD has allowed us to eat from, or we can touch the forbidden fruit of hatred. To hate someone is to be fully and unapologetically in opposition of GOD. It is to oppose HIM absolutely, for HE is love. It is to oppose HIS will for the person or people who hurt us. With hatred, comes the spirit of jealousy provoked by wrath and anxiety, and this leads to murderous thoughts. Anxiety is brought on by being anxious, and not wanting to wait on GOD to avenge us.

How is it that jealousy provokes a man to hatred? What if you hate the man because he murdered someone you love? Jealousy doesn't always mean that you want some material thing someone else has. Jealousy is when you want to take something from someone else because you don't think they are deserving of it, and that something could be their life. You don't want them to live, and you want to take their life from them; therefore, you are operating in jealousy. In this, you also display jealousy towards GOD. How so? You are attempting to sit in HIS place of judgment, where you condemn and pronounce judgment against another person. You then act as executioner to exact revenge against someone who's crossed you or someone you love. In killing them, you can't bring that loved one back, but you killed them to pacify the wrath that has been stirred up in you. Wrath often sits in a man when that man sits on GOD'S throne in his own heart. That's why GOD told us that vengeance is HIS. In other words, get out of HIS seat. Vengeance is like the King's staff; it is only to be held by HIM, but when you sit on HIS throne, you will put your hands on what belongs to HIM and it's too heavy for us to carry. That's also why GOD told us to be angry, but do not sin. "Be angry, and sin not: let not the sun go down upon your wrath: Neither give place to the devil" (Ephesians 4:26-27). Always remember that Satan envies GOD and wants to sit on HIS throne. If he can get into your heart and convince you to sit on GOD'S throne, he is vicariously sit on the throne of GOD through you.

Cain didn't murder Abel for his offering. He could have easily offered up the same thing. Cain murdered Abel because he was angry that his offering had not been accepted by GOD, but Abel's offering was. The Bible said Cain became wroth with GOD, which means he was filled with wrath towards GOD. He didn't want to be Abel; he wanted to take Abel's life in his wrath, and this is evidenced in his communications with GOD after he killed Abel. "And Cain talked with Abel his brother: and it came to pass, when they were in the field, that Cain rose up against Abel his brother, and slew him. And the LORD said unto Cain, Where is Abel thy brother? And he said, I know not: Am I my brother's keeper?" (Genesis 4:8-9). Jealousy provokes wrath, and wrath often leads to murder. As you can see, when Cain was questioned about his brother, the very first thing he did was to lie. He said he didn't know where Abel was, and this was a lie.

We must always get to the root of our lying; otherwise, we'll cut down the obvious, and the not-so-obvious will remain. One of the very first things we absolutely have to do is get rid of the lies that we've stored up in us. Lies attract more lies, and until you've rid your heart of the lies that you have believed in, you will continue to attract and be attracted to lies and liars. This is why confession is needed. Begin to confess every lie as a lie; renounce it and repent of it.

Next, ask the LORD to show you the lies that are in you so you can renounce them. Remember, you have a choice: You can open your heart and let the Truth in, or you can keep your heart closed and let the lies break your heart in an attempt to flee from the Truth.

Finally, you must tell the truth at all times. When you find that it hurts to tell the truth, please know that a haughty spirit is in your midst, and it should be rebuked. It doesn't necessarily mean that the haughty spirit is in you. It could mean that it's attempting to seduce you through your thoughts, and that's why GOD told you to cast down imaginations that exalt themselves against HIM. "Casting down imaginations, and every high thing that exalteth itself against the knowledge of God, and bringing into captivity every thought to the obedience of Christ..." (2 Corinthians 10:5). The "high thing" mentioned in this scripture is pride and any force (demonic) that is challenging the Truth.

After you've confessed the lies and

renounced them, begin confessing your sins daily so they won't store up in your heart. Confess how you feel to GOD every time you encounter a negative feeling, and stay away from liars. Anytime we associate with liars, we try to match them, and we too become liars. In order to keep dealing with them, we must walk and agree with them.

Always remember that anytime you feel pride, there is a lying spirit somewhere that the haughty spirit is guarding. Rebuke and bind them both. Additionally, stay away from people who entice you to sin. Surround yourself with wise men and women; individuals who love GOD and hate sin.

Proverbs 13:20: "He that walketh with wise men shall be wise: but a companion of fools shall be destroyed."
Luke 10:19: "Behold, I give unto you power to tread on serpents and scorpions, and

over all the power of the enemy: and
nothing shall by any means hurt you."
Psalm 1:1: "Blessed is the man that
walketh not in the counsel of the ungodly,
nor standeth in the way of sinners, nor
sitteth in the seat of the scornful."

Learning to Tell the Truth

It is difficult for a liar who has become accustomed to lying and comfortable with lying to tell the truth. There are people out there who simply don't know how to have a conversation without lacing it with lies. At the same time, most of us were brought up in lies and raised by liars; therefore, lying has become second-nature to us. So how do we tell the truth in a world full of lies and liars?

One of the first things we must do is confess the truth to ourselves. Oftentimes, we become so inundated with lies that we can no longer distinguish a lie from the truth. That's why the Bible says that many are walking in darkness. At the same time, the Bible refers to the LORD as the light of the world. It's amazing that we can hide the truth from ourselves, and in most cases, this is done because of pride. Most of us do not want to accept the truth about our failures, so we find creative ways to cover them up, but when we cover them, we begin to lie to ourselves. Like sugar, lies are addictive, and once we've received one lie, we'll crave another one and another one until we become addicted to receiving and telling lies. For example, you will witness those parents who believe everything their children say, and you'll notice that their children are compulsive liars. That's because their children were not corrected nor were they disciplined, but they've learned how to master lying. Lying becomes a first or second language to them. They become addicted to telling lies, and their parents become addicted to overlooking those lies. Children like this often grow up to become extremely perverted adults because lies have perverted their ways of thinking; nevertheless, their parents continue to defend them.

The next thing we should do is confess the truth to GOD. Please understand that HE already knows the truth, but when we've been bound by lies, we have to free ourselves by casting those burdens upon the LORD willfully. You'll find that it is especially hard to confess the truth to GOD because you have avoided accepting how deeply wrong your way of thinking is. Most of us feel that in telling GOD the truth, we are volunteering to be punished, but this is not true. In being truthful to GOD, we are telling HIM that we want to change, and we are acknowledging that we were wrong. If you find it difficult to verbalize the truth to GOD, try writing it down as a note to HIM and then reading it aloud in your alone time. There is no secret hidden from GOD, so don't be afraid to tell HIM what you've done. After you begin to confess the truth to HIM, you will find yourself feeling even more unburdened, and after a while, confessing your sins to HIM will become a habit to you. You will love the feeling of being unburdened and having yokes removed from your life. After you've learn to walk without burdens, you will never want to go back to being burdened. Tell GOD everything you're afraid and ashamed to tell HIM. Confess your sins; renounce your sins, and repent of your sins.

Finally, we must confess our sins to one another. If you've lied to someone, contact them and tell them the truth. It may seem scary at first, but once you've done this, you will see how freeing it is, and how rewarding it feels. At the same time, you unburden them from the lies they've received from you. Don't worry about how they will perceive you; worry more about displeasing GOD.

Learning to Tell the Truth

One of the things you can do to remain free
is to confess your sins, thoughts and fears
to GOD every night before going to bed.
The goal is to make a habit of being
truthful, and to learn to hate lies. GOD
wants us to love what HE loves and hate
what HE hates. One of the ways we do this
is by filling ourselves with the WORD of
GOD, and opposing anything that goes
against the WORD. At the same time, we
must have an intimate relationship with
HIM. Just religiously praying and reading
one's Bible isn't enough. We have to speak
to HIM personally and intimately. We must
speak to HIM in a way that signifies that we
know HE is real, and that HE hears us.
The more we get to know HIM, the more
we will love HIM. "If ye love me, keep my
commandments" (John 14:15).

One of the most obvious things that we
must do is separate ourselves from liars
indefinitely. There is no way around it; we

cannot sit in the seat of scorners, nor are we to associate with the workers of iniquity. Sure, we love them and we want to see them change, but that's a choice they have to make for themselves. If that liar happens to be your spouse, of course, you can't walk away from them unless GOD tells you otherwise. The proper thing to do is continue to lead by example, and love GOD with your whole heart. In doing so, you cause the unbeliever to come to a crossroads where they will have to choose between continuing to dwell with you and the GOD you serve or to walk away. Sure, we love our spouses and we oftentimes don't want them to walk away, but it is better for us to maintain our relationships with the LORD than it is for us to maintain our relationships with man. In obeying GOD, we are handing our spouses over to GOD to be corrected or judged. We can't change other human beings, but we can place them in GOD'S unchanging hands.

Learning to Tell the Truth

"So then neither is he that planteth any thing, neither he that watereth; but God that giveth the increase" (1 Corinthians 3:7).

Another tool that we must have is knowledge and understanding. If you don't understand what a lie is, what a lie does and why you shouldn't tell lies, you will eventually return to what you know. Study scriptures that speak against lying throughout the Bible, and read HOLY SPIRIT inspired books that teach against lying. What you are doing is actively coming against that lying spirit that may have found its way into your heart.

Lastly, you must enjoy your daily bread, which is the WORD of GOD. Read your Bible daily, and if you will, read it two or more times a day. Schedule a time to read the Bible. For example, you can read it before going to bed at night and before getting out of bed in the morning. In doing this, you are taking the Truth in, and opening yourself up to receive HIM. This makes it easier for us to reject the lies because in opening our hearts for the Truth, the lies don't have to break our hearts to get out of our hearts. "Behold, I stand at the door, and knock: if any man hear my voice, and open the door, I will come in to him, and will sup with him, and he with me" (Revelation 3:20).

The Pride Detector Test

It's not difficult to see if you've been imprisoned by pride. As a matter of fact, you will witness pride in your everyday dealings if your eyes are open. You have to learn to come against the haughty spirit behind pride so that you can walk a blameless life before the LORD.

A haughty spirit is always present to guard a lying spirit. If you find a person with a lying spirit, you have also found a person with a haughty spirit. But rather than testing others, it is always good to test ourselves for anything unholy, so we can cast those burdens upon the LORD. In conducting self-deliverance, what you'll find is that your mind will continue to change, and your associations will also change as your mind changes. You won't desire to hang out with the same people or do the same things.

Below are a few questions to ask yourself. If you feel discomfort or anger rising up in you when you attempt to answer these questions truthfully, you need to bind up the haughty spirit and the lying spirit. You may also need to bind rage and jealousy.

1. Think of someone you were romantically involved with in your past. Make sure the person is the one you were the most in love with. Are you still in love with them or would you give them a second chance if permitted? Why or why not?

2. Have you truly forgiven everyone who has hurt or betrayed you? Think about the person who did the worst harm to you. What would you like to

see happen to them right now? Be truthful with yourself.

3. Who do you fear? Don't be religious with your answers. Instead, list three people who you fear the most.

4. Whose success is intimidating to you? List two or three relatives or friends whose success you feel is intimidating.

5. Do you have a crush on someone close to you? Maybe a friend or a friend's spouse?

6. Do you consider yourself attractive or unattractive?

7. You're out walking and someone who is the same gender as you jogs by, bumps you and almost knocks you over. They don't apologize; instead, they scour at you, laugh, and then continuing jogging away. You see them jogging towards you the next day. How do you respond?

8. Your neighbor often called you ugly

when you were a child, and now you're a fully grown adult who happens to be quite attractive. You spot your neighbor at a restaurant just as the hostess is leading you to your seat, and she looks horrible. There's a spot open where she could get a clear view of you. Would you sit where the waitress asks you to sit, or would you request to be seated in the booth near the old neighbor?

9. You're married and your in-laws invite you to dine with them at a restaurant. You arrive thirty minutes early, and while pulling into the parking lot, you notice your spouse's ex walking into the restaurant. He or she is wearing the same outfit as you, and they look better in it. What would you do?

10. List five secrets you don't want anyone to know about.

The Pride Detector Test

There is a purpose for this line of questioning. You see, when dealing with a haughty spirit, some of those questions will bother you because many of your decisions and plans are based on how you perceive yourself and others. Therefore, in being truthful with yourself, you are forced to reconsider your plans. Oftentimes, these are plans that you've had in your heart for years, and it's hard to distance yourself from them, especially when you're left with a blank slate. Sometimes, we don't mind changing our plans if we have other plans to replace them with, but when we know we'll be left with a blank slate, we often fight to hold onto our plans. Most people will simply try to tweak their plans, rather than dismiss them.

Let's revisit each question so we can discern whether a haughty spirit is seducing you or not.

Think of someone you were romantically involved with in your past. Make sure the person is the one you were the most in love with. Are you still in love with them or would you give them a second chance if permitted? Why or why not?

- If the person in question has betrayed or hurt you, you will likely answer with a resounding "no" when pride has triggered unforgiveness in you. Unforgiveness is pride manifested as wrath, and anytime it is present, you will become bothered by any discussions of you reconciling with the person it's geared at. If you have forgiven them, and pride isn't present, you'd always be open for GOD'S will even if you don't understand it. Of course, if you are married, reconciling with an ex is out of the question. You'll notice that with people who have not wronged you and are not in bad standing with you, you would consider giving them another chance <u>if GOD said so</u>.

Have you truly forgiven everyone who has hurt or betrayed you? Think about the person who did the worst harm to you. What would you like to see happen to them right now? Be truthful with yourself.

- Again, unforgiveness is pride manifested as wrath. When we truly forgive people, our desires for them won't be to see them pay for what they've done to us. Our desires for them will be to see GOD'S will done in their lives, even if that means they repent of what they've done and go on to live a life full of blessings. When answering questions like this, it is rather hard to be truthful with one's self, because we are the first people we lie to. Try imagining your enemy blessed and living a great life.

Does that bother you? If it does, unforgiveness is present and that haughty spirit should be bound, rebuked and renounced.

Who do you fear? Don't be religious with your answers. Instead, list three people who you fear the most.

- We know that GOD tells us to fear no man; therefore, it is a sin to fear anyone but GOD. For this reason, we often hide fear in our hearts, rather than confronting it. We often hide fear behind pride, and this is especially true for men. If there is someone you fear, pride will likely tell you that you don't fear them, but you stay away from them for their own sake. Anytime you confront fear, you will come face-to-face with pride, and anytime you find pride, you'll find lies.

Whose success is intimidating to you?

List two or three relatives or friends whose success you feel is intimidating.

- Oftentimes we strive to be "better than" someone, rather than striving to be the "best at" something. For example, there is that son who feels that he must match or exceed his father's success. There is that sister who feels that she must outdo her sister to prove a point. Oftentimes, we see the success in others, and we strive to tip the scales in our favor, and this is prideful thinking. If you can think of two or three people who you feel the need to outdo, you need to come against that haughty spirit.

Do you have a crush on someone close to you? Maybe a friend or a friend's spouse?

- One thing about pride is that it stores up sin in our hearts. Now, in reading the question, you probably became offended at the thought of someone lusting after their friend's spouse. Nevertheless, this is not uncommon, and should be dealt with; otherwise, it becomes iniquity. Pride hides any lustful thoughts we have behind lies, because again, pride is a guarding spirit. Its purpose is to keep the person its leading from getting delivered. It's okay to be attracted to someone, but it's not okay to be romantically attracted to someone who is married. What's the difference? We see people all the time who we feel are attractive; meaning, they are pleasant to look upon. But to have a desire for that person is ungodly if that person is married or if you are married. If you find that you have a desire to be in a relationship with that person, or even a curiosity about what it would be like to be in a relationship with that person, humble yourself and repent. The best way to defeat a haughty spirit is by not giving it any hidden sins or iniquities to guard.

Do you consider yourself attractive or unattractive?

- How we perceive ourselves is often rooted in our understandings or misunderstandings. There are many people who have a wrongful and not-so-glamorous perception of themselves who will pridefully say that they love themselves and they feel beautiful or handsome. But in reviewing their choices in life, the truth peers from behind their words and declares them a liar. When a person feels unattractive, they don't always tell people because they don't want people to pity or minister to them. Pity makes them feel "diseased" or different. In addition, they don't want others to look down on them, so they'll lie to maintain a certain reputation with that person. When pride is on the scene, the person will often project a false sense of confidence, all the while leading a life that bears witness to their low self-perception.

You're out walking and someone who is the same gender as you jogs by, bumps you and almost knocks you over. They don't apologize; instead, they scour at you, laugh, and then continuing jogging away. You see them jogging towards you the next day. How do you respond?

- You're probably wondering why the example states that the offender is of the same gender as you. The truth is, we tend to be more prideful and confrontational of people of like genders. For example, if you're a

man and a lady bumps you, you're
likely not going to respond because
she's a lady. You know you're likely
too strong for her, and you've been
taught to never hit a woman. If
you're a woman and a man bumps
you, you'll likely respond by yelling at
him as he jogs away, but you'd let
the issue go without incident. Now, if
you're a man and another man
bumps you, you may read into his
behavior and want to respond
accordingly. Maybe he's challenging
you. Maybe he thinks you're weak.
Maybe he's showing off for some
women walking nearby.

If you're a woman and another
woman bumps you, you'll likely
respond with harsher words or you
may even engage her physically.
Maybe she's showing off for some
men or a man walking nearby.
Maybe she's jealous of you. Maybe

she thinks you're the woman who stole her husband from her. For whatever reason she bumped you, you'll likely respond to her faster than you would a man.

A haughty spirit usually responds to what we have in us whenever our triggers have been pulled. Using the example above, let's say that you're a man who had a horrible upbringing by your mother. Your perception of women has been altered by that relationship; therefore, if a woman was to bump you, you'd likely respond with harsh words. It's not that she bumped you that's so much of a bother; the issue is that she's a woman who bumped you. Always remember that anytime you witness a haughty spirit in action, it's guarding another spirit or several spirits. To get rid of the haughty spirit, you must humble yourself and confess whatever iniquity you have hidden in your heart.

Your neighbor often called you ugly when you were a child, and now you're a fully grown adult who happens to be quite attractive. You spot your neighbor at a restaurant just as the hostess is leading you to your seat, and she looks horrible. There's a spot open where she could get a clear view of you. Would you sit where the waitress asks you to sit, or would you request to be seated in the booth near the old neighbor?

- If you are pride-filled, you will likely say you'd sit wherever the hostess led you to, but in your heart, you know you'd try to make yourself seen by that old neighbor. One thing you'll witness with this line of questioning is that pride always leads you to lie to protect your own perception of yourself. How do you know when you're about to lie, or you're considering lying? When you have to think too hard about your answer. If you'd go out of your way to be seen, it's because you haven't forgiven that old neighbor, and you are still responding to what they said and who they were, as opposed to who they are now. We don't always respond with our mouths. Oftentimes, we respond to others through our actions. Pay attention to yourself and your decisions, and ask yourself, "What are my thoughts and choices responding to?"

You're married and your in-laws invite you to dine with them at a restaurant. You arrive thirty minutes early, and while pulling into the parking lot, you notice your spouse's ex walking into the restaurant. He or she is wearing the same outfit as you, and they look better in it. What would you do?

The Pride Detector Test

- The average person would turn
  around, go back home and change
  clothes because pride wouldn't let
  them exit their vehicles peacefully.
  In this scenario, the issue is jealousy
  and a need to win the battle of the
  beauties. One issue that many have
  is forgiving their spouse's exes for
  being their exes. Sure, it sounds silly
  but jealousy oftentimes presents
  itself when a soul tie is still present.
  If no soul tie is there, we'd likely enter
  the restaurant and not worry about
  the ex. How is it that you could have
  a soul tie with your spouse's ex? It's
  simple. When they lied down with
  them, they became one. If they
  hadn't been delivered from that soul
  tie before becoming one with you,
  then you are all members of one
  body. "Know ye not that your bodies
  are the members of Christ? Shall I
  then take the members of Christ, and

make them the <u>members</u> of an harlot? God forbid. What? Know ye not that he which is joined to an harlot is one body? For two, saith he, shall be one flesh" (1 Corinthians 6:15-16).

List five secrets you don't want anyone to know about.

- We all have something we have hidden in our hearts at some point or another out of humiliation, and it was hard to bring these things to public knowledge. Say them aloud. What are five secrets that you have? One thing you'll find is that pride will often keep you from opening your mouth, even when you are physically alone.

In answering all of the questions above, you should have paid attention to how you felt. Pride is always an indicator that lies are present in you; therefore, anytime you rebuke a lying spirit, you should also rebuke a haughty spirit. A lying spirit always comes with a haughty spirit, and a haughty spirit opens up our hearts for lying spirits to enter. If you've detected the haughty spirit as a stronghold in your mind, don't beat yourself up. Most people are guarded by haughty spirits. To rid yourself of this wicked devil, you should always remain humble and in submission to GOD. Confess your sins as soon as you realize them, and repent of them immediately. Think of it this way: If you had an ant problem in your home, and you called an exterminator, he'd come in and spray your home. After he's finished spraying, he'd tell you what to do to keep those insects out. Ridding yourself of demonic oppression works the same way. Sure, we can easily be free, but remaining free is the challenge. "When the unclean spirit is gone out of a man, he walketh through dry places, seeking rest; and finding none, he saith, I will return unto my house whence I came out. And when he cometh, he findeth it swept and garnished. Then goeth he, and taketh to him seven other spirits more wicked than himself; and they enter in, and dwell there: and the last state of that man is worse than the first" (Luke 11:24-26).

Because devils can't possess believers, they often oppress believers. Since they can't get into our hearts, they often try to find their ways into our minds. You see, when they could get into the heart of a man, they could control how he thinks. But when they can't reside in the heart, they go after the mind. A devil will introduce a thought to a man over and over again until he finally receives that lie in his heart. Once it's in his heart, it begins to alter the way he thinks, causing him to destroy himself.

Proverbs 6:16-19: "These six things doth

the LORD hate: yea, seven are an abomination unto him: A proud look, a lying tongue, and hands that shed innocent blood, An heart that deviseth wicked imaginations, feet that be swift in running to mischief, A false witness that speaketh lies, and he that soweth discord among brethren."

Proverbs 4:23: "Keep thy heart with all diligence; for out of it are the issues of life."

Ephesians 4:22-27: "That ye put off concerning the former conversation the old man, which is corrupt according to the deceitful lusts; And be renewed in the spirit of your mind; And that ye put on the new man, which after God is created in righteousness and true holiness."

James 4:7: "Submit yourselves therefore to God. Resist the devil, and he will flee from you."

2 Corinthians 10:5: "Casting down imaginations, and every high thing that exalteth itself against the knowledge of God, and bringing into captivity every thought to the obedience of Christ..."

The Great I AM and You

Have you ever wondered why GOD refers to HIMSELF as the Great I AM? When you reject lies and fill up on the truth, you will learn more about yourself, so your speech will become more confident. GOD knows who HE is, but do you know who you are?

When GOD speaks, HIS WORD is established; therefore, HIS WORD is Truth. When HE refers to HIMSELF as "I AM," HE is identifying HIMSELF as Everlasting. HE is eternal, and HE will continue to exist for eternity. HE is the Great and Almighty GOD; the everlasting FATHER, and there is none like HIM. "I am Alpha and Omega, the beginning and the end, the first and the last" (Revelation 22:13).

The Great I AM and You

Throughout the Bible, you will witness GOD
saying to HIS people, "Believe me." Why
does HE have to say this to us? Because
false doctrine has entered into our hearts,
and we oftentimes struggle with which
doctrine we want to believe. GOD tells us
over and over again to believe HIM and to
trust HIM, but because of the falsehoods in
our hearts, we tend to go from one belief to
another. GOD tells us to believe HIM
because HE is the Great I AM. What this
means is that HE exists always, and HIS
WORD will continue to stand. To believe
GOD is to receive GOD, but to not believe
HIM is to reject HIM. "So shall my word be
that goeth forth out of my mouth: it shall not
return unto me void, but it shall accomplish
that which I please, and it shall prosper in
the thing whereto I sent it" (Isaiah 55:11).

Everything that GOD says is already
established the moment HE speaks it.
When GOD said "Let there be light," the

138

Bible tells us that it was so. GOD is HIS WORD, and HIS WORD is who HE is; therefore, when HE speaks, whatever HE has spoken begins to exist immediately, and this is why HE is the Great I AM.

But just who are you? We oftentimes struggle with our identities, because we've been taught that we should fit into a specific group or category. Growing up, we tried on many identities; especially those of our favorite celebrities. We dressed like our favorite celebrities; we spoke like them, and we tried to wear our hair like them. We were lost and did not know who we were back then. Nowadays, we are adults, and many of us still don't know who we are, so we continue to try on identities. We enter friendships and begin to channel the behaviors of our friends, oftentimes unknowingly. We enter relationships and we begin to change for the sake of maintaining those relationships. We learn what our partner expects from us, and we try to meet their expectations of us. We are a people who look for clues as to who we are in other people.

What most people don't know is that who we are is hidden in GOD. The further we go in the WORD, the more we will discover who we are. When the WORD of GOD enters us, it shines its light in us, revealing the answers to those questions we've had all of your lives. The more we seek the face of GOD, the more we will find out about ourselves. In addition, when we seek the knowledge of GOD, GOD will continue to add onto us because we are showing ourselves as trustworthy vessels of GOD. "His lord said unto him, Well done, good and faithful servant; thou hast been faithful over a few things, I will make thee ruler over many things: enter thou into the joy of thy lord" (Matthew 25:23).

The Great I AM and You

To get to know you better, you must first release who you've learned to be. Additionally, you will have to walk away from the people who've learned to identify with the old you, but cannot accept who GOD has created you to be. Most people who came in your life when you were in your hours of blindness, are there because they too were blind. Once GOD begins to clean up your mind, they may no longer walk with you because the two of you may no longer agree with you. "Can two walk together, except they be agreed?" (Amos 3:3).

When we give ourselves to the LORD, we are giving ourselves back to our CREATOR. Because HE is our CREATOR, HE knows what tweaks we need to cause us to operate at our maximum potential in the realm of the earth. "A new heart also will I give you, and a new spirit will I put within you: and I will take away the stony heart out of your flesh, and I will give you a heart of flesh" (Ezekiel 36:26).

Truthfully, you'd be amazed to discover the greatness that lives within you. Most people never tap into this greatness because most people exist in certain mindsets, and they have no desire to elevate out of their ways of thinking. There is so much in us that the majority of us will never tap into because we often fear what's on the other side of what we don't know. We are creatures of comfort who don't like to be moved out of our comfortable places. We find mindsets and we try to nest there for a lifetime. We must be willing to embrace new realities as we discover the wholeness of GOD and the mysteries of GOD. Sure, this means that we will walk away from old lifestyles; we will give up old ways of thinking, and we will have to let go of some of the relationships that we've grown comfortable with, but discovering the fullness and wholeness of GOD is a wonderful journey that's worth everything that it costs.

Largely Ignored Truths

There are many truths that we as believers have come to ignore or reject, but denying the truth doesn't not discredit or overthrow the truth.

1. Some people say that GOD and JESUS are one and the same. Others say that GOD and JESUS are not the same. What is the truth? The truth is, CHRIST JESUS is the living WORD of GOD manifested in the flesh. HE is a part of the tri-fold: YAHWEH (JEHOVAH), YESHUA (CHRIST JESUS), and the HOLY SPIRIT. When the Bible says the WORD was with GOD and the WORD was GOD, what the Bible is saying is that GOD is HIS WORD. You cannot separate GOD from HIS WORD, for the two are one. When GOD created man,

HE formed man from the dust of the ground. With CHRIST, however, HE was spoken into existence, for HE is and was HIM who is to come and who has come. HE is the living WORD of GOD; therefore, HE is one with GOD, but HE operated in the flesh with HIS own will. HE chose to do the will of GOD. GOD gave HIM the ability to operate as a man, and to make choices without being controlled by GOD. The scriptures make it evident that CHRIST operated in HIS will.

Luke 22:41-42: "And he was withdrawn from them about a stone's cast, and kneeled down, and prayed, Saying, Father, if thou be willing, remove this cup from me: nevertheless not my will, but thine, be done."

John 5:30: "I can of mine own self do nothing: as I hear, I judge: and my judgment is just; because I seek not mine own will, but the will of the Father which hath sent me."

John 6:38: "For I came down from heaven, <u>not to do mine own will</u>, but the will of <u>him that sent me</u>."

The religious argument that emerges about whether or not GOD and CHRIST are the same is rooted in a lack of understanding and a failure to search the scriptures. GOD is HIS WORD, and the WORD became flesh and lived amongst mankind. The WORD operated as a man in HIS own will, yet HE chose to do the will of GOD. Isaiah 55:11 tells us a little more about the WORD. "So shall my word be that goeth forth out of my mouth: it shall not return unto me void, but it shall accomplish that which I please, and it shall prosper in the thing whereto I sent it." When CHRIST walked in the earth, HE accomplished everything that HE was sent by GOD to accomplish. Again, HE is the living WORD of GOD.

2. Man cannot live by bread alone, but by every word that proceeds out of the mouth of GOD. (See Matthew 4:4). Cancer, diabetes, high blood pressure and other infirmities are often linked to the foods we eat. The average believer does not read the Bible often; therefore, the average believer is in the dark. Because of this, many believers walk around claiming whatever reports their doctors have given them. Some even claim diseases and infirmities after watching commercials that give the symptoms of certain ailments. This is why we need the WORD in us. When the WORD comes in, there is no room for us to receive any other doctrine.

3. The devil needs permission to attack a believer who resides in the WORD, but a double-minded person is not standing on the WORD of GOD; therefore, GOD will oftentimes hand them over to their sin. When the devil wanted to attack Job, he

had to ask GOD'S permission. When the devil wanted to sift Peter, he had to ask GOD'S permission. But when Ahab was serving Baal, GOD gave a lying spirit permission to deceive him so that he would go into battle against Ramoth Gilead and be killed. "And even as they did not like to retain God in their knowledge, God gave them over to a reprobate mind, to do those things which are not convenient; Being filled with all unrighteousness, fornication, wickedness, covetousness, maliciousness; full of envy, murder, debate, deceit, malignity; whisperers, Backbiters, haters of God, despiteful, proud, boasters, inventors of evil things, disobedient to parents, Without understanding, covenant-breakers, without natural affection, implacable, unmerciful: Who knowing the judgment of God, that they which commit such things are worthy of death, not only do the same, but have pleasure in them that do them" (Romans 1:28-32).

4. Many believers are afraid of the devil
and his angels, but the devil is also afraid
of a believer who knows the WORD. The
enemy is empowered by fear because fear
demonstrates the lack of faith. Anytime a
devil is empowered by fear, it will continue
to terrorize the person who fears it.
"Submit yourselves therefore to God.
Resist the devil, and he will flee from you"
(James 4:7). Always remember that the
devil only has as much power as you give
him.

5. Most marriages don't end because of
infidelity; most marriages end because of
lies. When a person becomes a liar, he or
she will unleash havoc against their
marriage with their own words. Most
marriages could survive infidelity if the
offender was repentant and truthful, but the
majority of marriages that do end, end
because the offended spouse can no
longer trust the offending spouse.

Surprisingly enough, some marriages even even after both parties remained monogamous with one another. Even though both parties were faithful to each another, the marriage ended because one spouse chased peace out of the house by telling countless lies and standing by those lies.

6. Teaching a child that Santa Claus, the Tooth Fairy and the Easter Bunny are real is setting that child up to stumble. Children should never see lies as acceptable in any situation. It's not godly, nor is it harmless.

7. Most American holidays are pagan, and most American Christians know this; nevertheless, many continue to celebrate because they've grown to love the celebrations. They also believe that participating in the celebration of these holidays is harmless to them and their children. After all, as many would say,

"GOD knows my heart." This statement is a sinner's national anthem.

8. Most believers have not separated themselves from the world as GOD has commanded, but they will separate themselves from any church or Christian who teaches absolute holiness. The term "holier than thou" is often used by believers who feel convicted by the presence, words or actions of another believer they perceive to be more righteous than themselves or a hypocrite.

9. Rejecting a messenger of the truth is the same as rejecting the Truth HIMSELF. Many believers think they can justify rejecting the messengers by highlighting the messenger's imperfections; nevertheless, we are held accountable for any truths we have rejected whether it came from a man or a donkey.
10. Most saints who marry sinners end up

in divorce court. Most saints who marry
sinners believe they can win their spouses'
souls for the Kingdom, but they eventually
discover why GOD warns us not to be
unequally yoked with unbelievers. Their
souls can be won, but it's rare, draining and
hurtful.

11. You can't be friends with someone who
hates your spouse, just as you can't be
friends with a world who hates your GOD.

12. The one person many believers forget
to forgive is themselves.

13. There is no such thing as a "white lie."
Every lie is from the doctrine of Satan, and
every liar will be held accountable for the
lies they've told.

14. A lie can cause you to spend twenty
years in a bad relationship that the truth
would have ended before it even started.

15. Most lies are rooted in fear, established in pride and guarded by offense.

16. A liar can speak the truth sometimes. It doesn't mean they are changing. It often means they are attempting to change you by being crafty.

Spotting a Liar

What's amazing is the world has established ways to detect when someone is telling lies. One of these tests is the lie detector test. The lie detector test measures a person's heart rate, breathing, pulse, blood pressure and perspiration. When a person lies, their heart rate, breathing, pulse and blood pressure usually increases. People who are lying also perspire more when being dishonest. Even though these tests are not one hundred percent accurate, they have been used in police interrogations around the world and have been known to flush out lies from countless liars. What is it about the human body that causes it to change when a person tells a lie? The answer is simple. We were not created to hold lies, tell lies or to process lies. We were created to worship GOD, and we must worship HIM in spirit and in truth.

Are there any tests that we can do, as believers, to distinguish a liar from someone who is speaking the truth? Here are a few tips below:

- Eye movement. Liars tend to move their eyes around a lot when lying. Why is this done? We can't truly focus when telling lies. We have to put a lot of thought into what we are saying, and most of us can't speak and think without being overly animated. All the same, there are some liars out there who can stand still and look you in the eyes while telling a lie.
- Excessive hand movement. Again, liars tend to be overly animated because they are having to think up

their stories in haste, or they have to remember the stories they told, and this isn't always easy.

- Aggressive responses. Liars tend to become aggressive with their words when their lies are being questioned. This is an attempt to intimidate the person who is seeking the truth.

- Overly emotional responses. Sometimes, liars cry in an attempt to appear honest. When someone speaks the truth, you will find that they are oftentimes persistent and firm, but not emotional.

- The liar's pursuit. Liars tend to follow the person they are lying to when they fear that their lies are about to be uncovered. Someone who is telling the truth will oftentimes walk away or stand still because they aren't worried about any lies being uncovered.

- Liars tend to repeat your words back

to you. For example, let's say you were married to a man who'd received an extra bonus check at work, but he lied to you about it. When questioning him, he will likely repeat some of what you've said to him because he's trying to buy time to come up with an answer.

- Liars will oftentimes not allow a conversation to die, but will try to badger the person who has been challenging their lies.

- Liars often stumble over their words because their mouths are trying to speak words faster than their minds can process new lies. Because of this, liars often retract their statements.

- Liars will often avoid the people they've been lying to, and they will attempt to avoid conversations about their lies.

- Liars tend to avoid and dislike people

whom they fear can expose them.

- Liars tend to become nervous as their heart rate increases. The most obvious sign that a liar has been cornered by the truth is the uncontrollable shaking of his or her hands. Handing a piece of paper to them will oftentimes reveal whether they are nervous or not.
- Liars will often end a conversation if they feel their lies will be exposed.
- The pitch in a liar's voice will often change when he or she is lying.

Of course, these aren't surefire ways to tell if someone is lying because every person is different; nevertheless, the average person's body language changes when they tell lies. It's easier to detect if someone is lying when you know the person and their habits. Most liars cannot and will not remain consistent and poised while telling lies.

10 Scriptures About Lying

Proverbs 6:16-19: "These six things doth the LORD hate: yea, seven are an abomination unto him:
* A proud look, a lying tongue, and hands that shed innocent blood,

* An heart that deviseth wicked imaginations, feet that be swift in running to mischief,

* A false witness that speaketh lies, and he that soweth discord among brethren."

Proverbs 19:9: "A false witness shall not be unpunished, and he that speaketh lies shall perish."

10 Scriptures About Lying

Colossians 3:9-10: "Lie not one to another, seeing that ye have put off the old man with his deeds; And have put on the new *man*, which is renewed in knowledge after the image of him that created him."

1 John 2:4: "He that saith, I know him, and keepeth not his commandments, is a liar, and the truth is not in him."

1 John 4:20: "If a man say, I love God, and hateth his brother, he is a liar: for he that loveth not his brother whom he hath seen, how can he love God whom he hath not seen?"

Psalms 101:7: "He that worketh deceit shall not dwell within my house: he that telleth lies shall not tarry in my sight."

John 8:44: "Ye are of *your* father the devil, and the lusts of your father ye will do. He was a murderer from the beginning, and abode not in the truth, because there is no truth in him. When he speaketh a lie, he speaketh of his own: for he is a liar, and the father of it."

Ephesians 4:25: "Wherefore putting away lying, speak every man truth with his neighbour: for we are members one of another."

Revelation 21:8: "But the fearful, and unbelieving, and the abominable, and murderers, and whoremongers, and sorcerers, and idolaters, and all liars, shall have their part in the lake which burneth with fire and brimstone: which is the second death."

1 John 4:1-6: "Beloved, believe not every spirit, but try the spirits whether they are of God: because many false prophets are gone out into the world. Hereby know ye the Spirit of God: Every spirit that confesseth that Jesus Christ is come in the flesh is of God: And every spirit that confesseth not that Jesus Christ is come in the flesh is not of God: and this is that spirit of antichrist, whereof ye have heard that it should come; and even now already is it in the world. Ye are of God, little children, and have overcome them: because greater is he that is in you, than he that is in the world. They are of the world: therefore speak they of the world, and the world heareth them. We are of God: he that knoweth God heareth us; he that is not of God heareth not us. Hereby know we the spirit of truth, and the spirit of error."